CONTENTS

Gardening is fun, but your hands will probably be dirty when you finish!

21st Century Junior Library

Practice Good Hygiene!

by Katie Marsico

CHERRY LAKE PUBLISHING * ANN ARBOR, MICHIGAN

CHERRY
LAKE
Publishing

Published in the United States of America by Cherry Lake Publishing
Ann Arbor, Michigan
www.cherrylakepublishing.com

Content Adviser: Charisse Gencyuz, M.D., Clinical Instructor, Department of Internal Medicine, University of Michigan.

Reading Adviser: Marla Conn, ReadAbility, Inc

Photo Credits: © Scott Rothstein/Shutterstock Images, cover; © Jenn Huls/Shutterstock Images, 4;
© pixinoo/Shutterstock Images, 6; © MANDY GODBEHEAR/Shutterstock Images, 8;
© Olesia Bilkei, 10; © Tatyana Vyc/Shutterstock Images, 12; © Jaimie Duplass/Shutterstock Images,
14; © bluebloodbkk/Shutterstock Images, 16; © Edyta Pawlowska/Shutterstock Images, 18;
© legenda/Shutterstock Images, 20

LIBRARY OF CONGRESS CATALOGING-IN-PUBLICATION DATA
Marsico, Katie, 1980-
    Practice good hygiene!/By Katie Marsico.
        pages cm.—(Your healthy body)
    Includes index.
    Audience: 6-10
    Audience: K to grade 3
    ISBN 978-1-63188-987-5 (hardcover)—ISBN 978-1-63362-065-0 (pdf)—
ISBN 978-1-63362-026-1 (pbk.)—ISBN 978-1-63362-104-6 (ebook)
    1. Hygiene—Juvenile literature. I. Title.
    RA777.M269 2015
    613—dc23   2014021527

Cherry Lake Publishing would like to acknowledge the work of
The Partnership for 21st Century Skills.
Please visit www.p21.org for more information.

Printed in the United States of America
Corporate Graphics

Why Wash Up?

Wow–Ali's hands have gotten so dirty! She's just finished working in the garden. Now she's starving. Grandma reminds her to clean up before dinner.

Think!

Think about the last time you washed your hands. Was the water you used clean? Did you use soap? Did you scrub the backs of your hands and under your nails? You should wash for about 20 seconds–as long as it takes to sing "Happy Birthday."

Washing your hands is one of the
easiest ways to stay healthy.

She says that hand-washing is an important part of practicing good hygiene. Ali needs a **routine** to keep her body and surroundings clean. This helps prevent illnesses from spreading.

People follow habits to care for their skin, hair, mouth, teeth, hands, feet, and nails. These habits help the body stay free of **bacteria** and other germs. Germs

Ask Questions! What are germs? How do they make you sick? Ask your nurse or doctor! Find out which good-hygiene habits you should practice to fight these organisms!

Good hygiene helps everyone
around you stay well, too.

are tiny **organisms** that create disease. Luckily, good hygiene makes it harder for germs to grow and spread.

Practicing good hygiene also gives you a neat, **well-groomed** appearance. Showering reduces sweat smells and other **odors**. Brushing teeth prevents bad breath.

Having good hygiene often boosts **self-esteem**. When Ali has clean hair, skin, and clothes, she feels proud of her body and more comfortable around other people. This improves her mood and her relationships.

Always wash your hands after handling a pet.

Basic Body Care

Ali heads to the sink after dinner. Grandma explains that people who practice good hygiene wash their hands several times a day. This includes before and after cooking, eating food, coughing, sneezing, using the bathroom, and touching pets.

Trimming your nails is also good hygiene. This prevents germs from building up

Washing your hair at least a few times a week
helps keep it shiny and strong.

underneath them. It reduces the risk of **infections** and **hangnails** as well.

Grandma says Ali's nails look well-trimmed. She notices how shiny and clean Ali's hair is, too. Ali says she washes it every other day, and brushes it often.

Ali also takes a bath every night. This stops dead skin **cells** from piling up. It also clears away dirt and oil that make her skin and hair greasy.

Bathing helps Ali fight body odor, too. So does wearing clean clothes. The

Brushing your teeth helps keep your mouth healthy.

bacteria on dirty, stained clothing can create unpleasant smells.

This is also true of bacteria found in a person's mouth. Such germs often cause bad breath, **cavities**, and gum disease. What can you do to reduce these bacteria? Brush your teeth at least twice a day. Floss your teeth at least once a day. These good-hygiene habits are what give Ali her bright, beautiful smile!

Dirty dishes often smell bad. They also make it easier for germs to spread.

Being Clean: The Big Picture

Ali helps Grandma load the dishwasher. Ali is surprised to learn that this is an example of good hygiene. Grandma explains that keeping everything around them clean keeps germs from spreading.

Look! Make a list of areas or objects that you use at home and school. Are these areas or objects clean and organized? Do you spot any possible hygiene problems? If so, are you able to figure out how to fix them?

When you have to blow your nose,
always use a tissue.

Good hygiene makes it more pleasant to spend time at home, school, and other places. Of course, that doesn't mean Ali enjoys cleaning her room. Still, she finds it easier to study and relax there when it's tidy.

Ali has learned many good-hygiene habits. She is trying to stay healthy. And she wants her surroundings to be clean and

Make a Guess!

It's good hygiene to cough or sneeze into a tissue or your arm. Can you guess why? Hint: Think about how germs spread.

Practicing good hygiene will help you
feel and look your best!

germfree. This improves life for everyone around her. For instance, hand-washing doesn't just help her avoid harmful bacteria. It also prevents her from passing germs to other people. Then Ali's family and friends are less likely to get sick.

Grandma has helped Ali understand how to make her new habits part of her routine at home. But it's not time for Ali to leave just yet. Grandma suggests they have some milk and cookies. But they have to wash their hands first!

GLOSSARY

bacteria (bak-TEER-ee-uh) simple organisms that sometimes cause disease

cavities (KAH-vuh-teez) holes in teeth that are caused by decay, or rot

cells (SELZ) the smallest units that make up living things

hangnails (HAYNG-naylz) small pieces of loose skin that hang along the bottoms and sides of fingernails and toenails

infections (in-FEK-shuhnz) illnesses caused by germs or viruses

odors (OH-duhrz) particular smells

organisms (OR-guh-nih-zuhmz) living things

routine (roo-TEEN) a regular way of doing things in a certain order

self-esteem (SELF-uh-STEEM) the feeling of having confidence and satisfaction in oneself

well-groomed (WELL-GROOMD) clean, tidy, and dressed well

FIND OUT MORE

BOOKS

Barraclough, Sue. *Wash and Clean*. Mankato, MN: Sea-to-Sea Publications, 2012.

Bellisario, Gina, and Holli Conger (illustrator). *Take a Bath! My Tips for Keeping Clean*. Minneapolis: Millbrook Press, 2014.

Lennon, Liz. *I Keep Clean*. Mankato, MN: Sea-to-Sea Publications, 2013.

WEB SITES

The Canadian Red Cross— Bug Out!

www.redcross.ca/crc /documents/3-1-3-2-1-Bug-Out-6-8 -Activity-Booklet.pdf
Download an activity booklet that provides more information on germs and how to beat them by using good hygiene!

Centers for Disease Control and Prevention— BAM! Body and Mind

www.cdc.gov/bam/body /index.html
Learn more facts about good hygiene, including how it helps to build a healthy body.

INDEX

ABOUT THE AUTHOR

Katie Marsico is the author of more than 150 children's books. She lives in a suburb of Chicago, Illinois, with her husband and children.